The Receiving Quilt

D1251824

Poems
Elissa Ann Cottle

To Rebecca,

An glad to have my poetry

in your hands!

With love,

Elissa

Up On Big Rock Poetry Series
SHIPWRECKT BOOKS PUBLISHING COMPANY
Minnesota

Shipwreckt Books Publishing Company
375 West 7th Street
Winona, Minnesota

for Jesse and Lucas
received with certain joy

The Receiving Quilt

Families of Origin

Morning in America

Red leaf hands
pull us out of sleep,

tap the window and there they are,
they climbed the ladders of fall,

like bits of flag, a country I could love,
pleading guilty for our crimes.

At daybreak the grass looks everything
like intention, morning dew on cold blades

of longing, the autumn-red branch speaking
drink in my own tongue of patriot.

Lake Harriet

The lake took me back again
and how could she resist?

I offered her my second born
and she gushed at the sight of him.

Lashes wet, brown eyes bigger than islands,
gladly in over his head.

The night after, I thanked her
with my own body.

In the dark, clothes dropped
on the cool sand, I walked in,

breasts swelling in their own
warm and generous water.

Rear View Mirror

Parked at the lake
to sip the scent of summer,

I lean my head
out the window,

and the top of my mother,
short waves of brown and gray,

shows up in the mirror,
unattached to the eyes of death.

I hold myself still,
not to startle her away.

When I pull my head back in,
I find her small hands

face up in my lap.

Cloth Diaper Towers

Mom was happy
when my brother arrived;
I was the little mother next to her.
She loved me for that.
We both adored the new boy,
blond wispy hair, light blue eyes.
A funny laugh.

Preparing food for the table was daunting
to Mom. But when my brother was born,
the dining room table
took on a grand new purpose.

It was the surface for dozens
of clean cloth diapers. They were white, soft
and more beautiful than any plate of food
that might emerge from a kitchen.

My job was to fold each warm diaper.
Perched on the wobbly wicker chair,
my skinny legs dangled, contented.

I built towers of folded diapers
on the table. I was doing something
important, making sure each fold
was straight, corners meeting corners
like destinations. The towers stood proud.
My mother was pleased.

She and I would bring Barton
out to the back yard and just gaze at him

as he wobbled in the grass.
He was the most beautiful thing I ever saw.

Better than that, my mother and I shared him,
like passing a sweet glass of lemonade
back and forth between us,
in the summertime of our lives.

The Bite

Blood spilled onto the white tiles of the floor.
He was a young boy, just 3, and we were cat people.

But in this bloody hour a dog galloped up the short
hill of our front yard
as if he had finally gnawed off the awful leash,

saw a small boy, his fine blond hair lifting
in the summer breeze,
his tender nose.

The dog bit the nose to the bone,
the tip hanging off his face by raw threads.

Nine years old, I took him into my skinny arms,
carried him upstairs to the bathroom,
both of us screaming,
awakening our mother.

The sight of all the blood made me dizzy;
I held onto the sink,
and can't remember what happened
after I stumbled away from the scene.

The nose was saved.
My brother would forever despise dogs.

From the Floor to the Roof

Mom likes to sit on the floor
below the dining room table,
leaning into the warm heat vent.
A cigarette, and phone cord, unravel up her arm
to her smoky blue mouth.

Sometimes she rises to the piano bench.
We're Jewish but she can make Handel
ring church bells out of our little house.

Sometimes Mom and I sit together
on the plain flat roof
of our garage in summer. Nothing is better.

We watch the neighbors walking below us
and laugh.

Families of Origin

Tami walks down the block to my house,
carrying her family.
Both of us 8 years old, we spread their perfect
bodies across the carpet in my pink room.
My family of 11. Hers 12.

My family was born at my birthday party
when I'm 5.
A present from a friend of my dad's.
When I unwrap the box, Barbie is packed
in a blue suitcase with her picture painted
on the outside.

Inside, she is waiting for me: tall, standing
on her tip toes, always ready for high heels.
A tiny nose and lips in a frozen kiss, with lipstick.
Dad is really happy for me. *I'd like one of those!*
People at the party laugh.

Her first dress is sparkly blue. But she needs
a husband, kids, pajamas, a coat, and a bed.
I save all my money to buy her Ken.

We throw a double wedding. Make invitations,
shop for wedding gowns and tuxedos.
There is real cake and photos.
The newlyweds drive to their honeymoon,
tops down on their convertible cars.

My family gets additions:
Skipper, Scooter, Rick, Tutti and more.
Tami and I have rules. Dinners served.
Kids home by 10.

In summertime, Mom shoos us outside.
So Tami and I relocate our families
to the interesting front patio,
designed by my dad, an architect, before he left.

We keep this going longer than other girls.
It stops when I'm 13 and meet a boy.

No Other Kiss

Was recorded in history until
you and I slid our backs
down a cool, concrete wall,
landing on unbeautiful gritty linoleum
in middle America.

You, a proper boy of the faith,
with an unbat mitzvahed 13-year-old girl.

Sunday was the day of our weekly affair
that lasted a good, long year.
Our fathers loaded us like an extra sport bag
into the back seat

of their smooth black cars,
packed with their racquets and hard rubber balls
and small vials of shampoo and deodorant.

We were hitching rides
to the scene of an original play every week.
One-acts of which we would never
speak to our fathers,
who gave us a perfunctory nod and half smile,

heading down into their dank white room
to crack those racquetballs
like the sound of gunshot in the basement
of the Jewish Community Center.

Community stirred throughout
the large-box building of rooms for sport
and art and gesticulating discussion
to sort out our place among gentiles.

But no one other than you and I
lived for our mouths to meet
on the after-sabbath day of our
long week of waiting.

An Education at Age 15

I have long brown hair, brown eyes, and I have Ross. We each catch the bus to meet downtown Minneapolis. His dad owns the Gay 90s, where he takes me for dates. It's a big, noisy place on Hennepin Avenue, where we watch glamorous women dance on a stage. (And, who knew, they turned out to be men!) People eat nice dinners in tall, red leather booths. Ross introduces me to everyone. They all love him and smile in approval of me. Sometimes Ross does the dishes in the back. He likes to go to the bar so he can see his dad. His family has a big house in the suburbs. His mom plays mahjong. My mom hangs out in Coffman Union, writing papers with her boyfriend, Reginald. When we're old enough to drive, Ross picks me up and we like to end up at Perkins late at night, where we sit in our favorite orange vinyl corner booth. We laugh and sometimes share a cigarette across the table. Ross plays the guitar and we listen to Joni Mitchell and Carole King in his bedroom for hours on Sunday afternoons. My friends want to know why I like him. He's loud and wears those big platform shoes and wide silver rings. His dad owns a gay bar and my dad is an architect. But I argue that Ross's dad gives gay people a place to feel accepted. You could call his dad a social worker.

Crossing the River

for Dawn Cottle, 1937-1991

and Phebe Hanson, 1928-2016

A bus stopped at a corner that was important
to the neighborhood; there resided
green chocolate-mint ice cream,
15-cent scoops of sublime in my mouth.

One day my mother rose and
waved down the orange summer bus toward me.
It was taking young artists to meet teachers
in their fields of desire.

For my 15th summer, it was all her doing:
I've found a place you can take your poems
across the river without me.

I looked out the window watching the shinier city
pass into the older bricks and mortar.
I met my poet laureate there.
She was issuing poems like fresh mint leaves,

as she stood in the warm grass
of the campus square, before our field of faces
tilted toward the blue, blue window of summer.

She took us back to when she was her daddy's girl.
Sitting straight in the country pew,
wool pink coat and round hat,
his voice bigger than a church room of windows.

She needed no podium
to show the preacher how it was.
She lived and lived, past him
and past my mother's grave.

She could bend the wind of voice.
My mother must have known.
It's the instrument born
and rising out of the body at dawn.

Then a Shoe Flew Past the Couch

Somewhere in Providence, my lover is making
shellfish crepes, spooning them beautifully
onto a nice restaurant plate.

It's late, it's 1979, I am 19 and wanting something
to say when he comes home from work
at midnight, tossing his chef apron into the wash.

The Cable Car of Providence is a *theatre with couches*,
says the box office recording.
(I call more than once. With couches?)

Curled on my couch, our preview is a juggler.
He steps in front of the screen and winks.
I remove a shoe, throw it into the fray.
Things fly in circles of three.
His hat travels love seat to sofa, collecting tips.

The film is Wertmuller's *The End Of The World
In Our Usual Bed In A Night Full Of Rain*.
We recline, watch Giannini and Bergen
draw out their seduction, Italy to San Francisco.

As he winds up the reel, the man behind
the projector asks me to follow him to a bar
for conversation. Why not?
He didn't lie about the couches.

I drive behind him in my car
along the skinny streets of Main, of Hope,
until he stops under a freeway bridge,
next to a piano bar.

No regrets, sings a woman at the piano
in an open window, purple neon,
in the silver voice of Phoebe Snow
flying into the dark.

But he walks me in the other direction,
toward a windowless ruin of concrete.
Inside, it's packed with live talkers.

I drive home with a story in my bag.

Our usual mattress sits
in the middle of the one-room rented flat,
in an old house with tall windows. The streetlamp
throws light on my night cook's face.

The rain is music in our new year.
Rapt, his elbow teeters on my knee,
listening to my night of couches and flying shoes.

His brow furrows,
searching for something to report.
He tells me the Shah has fled to Los Angeles.
I couldn't be happier.

New Music

Mother and son peer between tall grass
at the humming lake, silent.

The talk between lake walkers
drifts past their backs.

Standing behind him,
her hand rests on the yellow t-shirt
enclosing the 3-year-old shoulder.

I love you, he says, the first time,
tossing the words toward the water,

three piano notes plunking in,
composing a new piece of music.

An audience of ducks pedals by,
listening in their small, green pleasure boats.

for Jesse

Fourteen Weeks

You entered without a noise.
No greeting, just aches for more milk, more food

than I would usually put on a plate. In a day,
in an hour. Then I knew you were in.

Reeling yourself in, tiny ball turning the thread
of itself over and over. Toward the first child,

who would make space for you in a yellow room.
Toward more than a poem.

Blood prints, silent drip on your way out.
Seven weeks toward me, seven leaving.

No coffin, no hands, but for those holding on
to the edge of a dry table.

Winter Solstice

In a church room lit by candles,
we bring gifts to the table.
Drop our names in a bowl.

I choose one and my own name
opens like an eyelid.
Sarong, sarong, calls the gift
I wrapped for someone needing beauty

like the ballerina who collapses
and returns in one motion.

Batik sarong, it speaks in color,
deep from the canyon of color:
paprika, basil leaf, red onion, rusty clay.

So many cloths to clothe a life: the curtain,
the canopy, the bread towel, the bandage.
Hanging cloth on a wall covers
tiny holes of damage.

In the eye of the tailor's needle,
breasts shape pleats into small hammocks.
The batik cloth lifts a painted eyebrow—

there, in a river, a woman clothed
alone in a blue boat is saving her own life.

Fertility in Las Trampas, New Mexico

This town is a dip in the mountains,
founded 300 years ago by a dozen families
making a living off what they caught in fish traps.

Adobe church still rises like bread.
Floor boards tethered in clay.
Two planks make a cross
hanging flat on its back by a rope,

chandelier of plain-face white candles.

Across the road another church sells
God's accessories.
The priest stands behind the cash register.

I tell him I have one boy. And wanting.
He has just the thing.

The kokopelli comes home with me in a plane.

It does not flinch as a soul leaves its wooden body,
bent in a dance step. Does the trick.

The Window to Lake Superior in Cabin 4

The waves stir silky air in my lungs,
like my sons have done since they began.

One July, listening to the sounds of the lake,
the first boy and I sleep
in the cabin bed, his arms around the baby,

who is unrolling in my belly between us.
The following July the baby is introduced

to the old, undying waves. Huge, gray rocks
always devoured and reborn by water.
If there were seat belts

on the rocks I would set him down on one,
admire him from a short distance, like a painting.

In front of the window, tabletop, he is tilted upright
in his miniature hammock, safely strapped in.

Already minding the water.

This lake hurls to my shore asking is there anything
more I can give you.

It rides in, under these waves,
hits the shore, then backs out on its knees.

At home I ask the kitchen to heat the writing water.

Without asking, the light lays down its late
afternoon design across our old oak floor.

for Lucas

Man and Boy Laughing

after a photograph by Wing Young Huie

The white of diaper folds like linen
against the black cloth of new skin.

Flash in the man's mouth catches a smile
off the boy. When the boy laughs,

it shakes a funny soul out of our body
like the day he was born.

Wing sees it. The city's Central neighborhood,
boy's hip snug
against man's on their front stoop. Boy's hand
resting on man's leg.

Wing Huie, young artist,
blows the image building size,
posts it on the boarded-up Sears tower.

Man and Boy Laughing down Lake Street.
Woman sees it—wants that laugh
in her living room.

Man's hand on his knee.
Bit of cigarette loose between his fingers.
Smoke nearly invisible in summer light.

Long silver-cross necklace pauses
against man's flat belly.
Heart inked on a bicep.

Boy's legs cross at the ankle,
squeezing an extra smile out of his feet.
Sun shines on his forehead curve. Joy on lower lip.

My copy in silver-leaf frame,
posted on the wall above the old upright.
Five-dollar miniature bust of Mozart on piano top.

Son on the bench plays classical, then jazz.

Man and boy laugh
above white plastic head of Mozart.
Mozart unable to crack a smile.

"Man and Boy Laughing" was first displayed, 8' wide by 12' tall, on the street level of the old Sears tower in Minneapolis. It was among 675 black and white photographs posted on building exteriors in Wing Young Huie's celebrated 6-mile exhibition, "Lake Street USA, 1997 – 2000." The Sears tower is now anchored by the Midtown Global Market at Lake Street and 10th Avenue South.

Four Originals

There is no neon sign sticking its neck out
for Big V's on University, Midway St. Paul.
Just a cigarette blinking orange, on and off,
from the lips of a bartender
taking a break on the sidewalk.

Black leather jacket squares my small shoulders
for occasions just like this.
A man aging about my pace
straddles his extra weight over a bar stool.
Five-dollar cover, he says, rubber stamping the top
of my wrinkled hand.

I edge past pool tables,
thin tops stretched across pairs of breasts,
lines like apples in summer. In the back,
I spot my dates: the ex and his wife.

It's his wife I am drawn to in these situations.
I love this wife and mother
we all wish we had.
Fresh basil pesto and warm brownies.
Loves my son when he is under their roof.

Our boy, 15, steps onto the stage.
Bass slung low over the front of his hips,
his dad's rusty hair spraying around his face.
Black bandana across his forehead.
Large black X drawn
below his knuckles—no alcohol for this hand.

Four originals and six covers,
Mom, he told me earlier in the day,
as I stood outside the bathroom doorway,
watching him apply stiff gel into his hair,
cut fresh by the Uptown Hair Police.

The legal-age drummer and two vocalists
hold up their shots to toast their live debut
on stage. My kid cups his hand around
his invisible glass, meets their clink in the air.

I glance across the table at his dad
to see if he caught that. But he missed it,
enjoying his survey of the scene in total.

I put him back on the coffeehouse stage
25 years before in California.
Harmonica, red hair spiked.
He would sway me back and forth to music,
a high, grateful deadhead.

Our son's band is loud, and not bad.
Van Morrison, Bob Seger. Plus the originals.
In the middle of the set, he gets a guitar solo.
He's good.
Dad tosses a grin across the table to Mom.

"Your son is the best musician up there,"
a friend, also in a band, shouts into my ear.
I take her word for it,
and raise my glass to his stepmom and his old man.

The Year a Wizard Could
Not Stop a War But Won My Heart

after Stéphane Mallarmé's "A Throw of the Dice"

Once upon time the Land of Oz
commanded a delivery from my backyard:
the climbing castle of orange and blue slides.
Yellow castle tunnel
the boy snaked his way through,
all that beautiful, tough
plastic color in my wild trees.

Now he's the director of the show.
Hurl it in to seal the gap
on stage, he said, tall with vision.
Castle parts are dismantled,
carried away in a pickup,
become props to convince Dorothy
she has landed someplace slightly familiar.

x

Once something awful surged over the chief,
the one we loved
and elected to lead us out of the war.
He went 30,000 soldiers deeper,
sucked into the bloody mud.
Hurl of men seals nothing.
There is no castle to build there.
Oz hunkers behind the curtain.

x

I skipped along yellow bricks once.
Yellow tuxedo walking to my door
sounding like velvet crumpled by a dull guffaw.
You did say it would be yellow,
but how could I have pictured
yellow bow tie, yellow ruffle shirt, wrinkled
under yellow jacket, squeezed by yellow
cummerbund? You were the sunset,
the dance, the climb to the top of the hill,
our castle under stars,
funny yellow tuxedo in summer.

χ

An ordinary swell of window light
dilutes the darkened theater of boys
in green metal helmets. Raise the window shades,
new little son. Sit beside me
with your book as I read mine.
Let's start our lives over again today.

χ

A poet once said all thoughts
emit a throw of the dice.
Snow storm out the window flips into a sky of dice,
the show closes with roses
for Dorothy and her director,
the castle is hauled back to my yard in a pickup,
in pieces, unharmed.

Naming Rights

Swinging a leg over my bike,
I ride to Lake Harriet Elementary School,
named after Lake Harriet,
after Harriet Lovejoy Leavenworth.

Two centuries ago, Colonel Henry Leavenworth
was passing through
on his way to kill natives on the Plains.

Henry and wife Harriet
lived for a time at Fort Snelling,
and it was decided Harriet should have a lake.

Late tokens, but Confederate
statues finally are falling down.
Rather than bulldozing whole buildings,
names are torn off brick walls.

Parking my bike in the rack, I spot my
blond boy, 6 years old, arms in flight,
catching the sun on the school lawn
like he owns the place.

Six Abandoned Cabins
in Grand Marais

Each summer saying goodbye
to the lake and the hill,
Ben Franklin and the lighthouse,
I fold the splintery
cabin squares into my cotton clothing and toiletries.

Six small houses in a row on First Street,
pitched roof, rowboat-green paint chip.
Take them home. Plan to save them one day.

Entering the first one, I'll push open a door
already ajar, stand still in spider's dust,
in the long grass of time. Turn the contents over.

Dry mattress, petal blue sweater unraveling
along the wrist. Dull pot, curtain rod. Pillow cloth
asleep a hundred summers
but containing all the white feathers
of one loud, flapping spring.

The door releases itself from its hinges
in my hands like grief.
Glass in the windows resolves not to break.
Each wall stands
ready to shelter
at this moment of intended conception.

Unhinged Theater,
Southwest High School

for Matthew Shepard, 1976-1998

Mountain biker finds a body
tethered to the post, 18 hours, still breathing.
My son wears a jean jacket for the part:
biker who notices a scarecrow.

The biker's voice breaks,
thin cracker in his mouth, echo in the black box.

The local bartender wears a red cap,
one prop per part.
He remembers young Shepard:
21 years old, beautiful slanted jaw, fine blond hair.

The bartender testifies he saw Shepard
cozy up, on a bar stool,
next to Henderson and McKinney.
They said Shepard asked them for a lift home.

Climbed into their truck. Let his hand rest light
on the driver's leg. Set off their *gay panic* button—

a defense that gathers wind in the steeples
but does not save them.
The biker watches as the police untie the body,
which lives, unconscious, four more days.

My boy's hands mime rope
the color of prairie, that bends its wheat skulls
and spreads itself like prayer under a wide
Wyoming sky.

The Hundredth Day

Working in the sky
37 stories up, I am one woman

on my Target team, editing reports,
surrounded by my Target men.
One giggles.

It drifts above the cube next to mine,
song notes in the corporate hum of Target air.

Someone's son,
boy who grew up shedding all boyhood
we expect men to discard,
but for the giggle that latched on

to his pinstripe shirttail last minute,
before man broke away from boy.

Stowaway.

In this last year with my first boy at home,
I've been making preparations.
His small laugh, for example, is saved in voice mail.

Every 100 days, the laugh circles down to my ear
from the mail hidden in the sky.
To save, press nine, instructs the keeper of voice mail.

This message will be saved for one hundred days.
She makes this offer punctually.

Every hundredth day, for 10 years,
I have gratefully accepted the deal.

After work, I ask the grown man to show me
the skyway to my car.
We push through glass doors, pass enormous
red targets beaming off the walls.

Pass security into space where
skyway subs, smoothies and vitamins
hover like smaller stars circling the big three:

Target
        Macy's
US Bank

The man who giggles came to Target, Minnesota,
after he lost his marriage in Ohio.

Keeps returning to Ohio
to see the people who still love him.
Can't decide if he's here for good, or there.

From his apartment in the sky
it's just a short walk to work, he says with a laugh.
The apartment is even higher, he points, than the
37th shelf of Target Tower, where we live by day.

At night, he looks out over the blinking lights
of the city, I imagine,
that sound folded in his chest
like voice recorded, then saved.

You Asked Me to Send
the Bowie Poster

Bowie peels slow off the burnt-orange wall
of your room.

He scrolls like a torah across the dining room table,
to be delivered to your new door,
conservatory for theatre in Montreal.

Of course they wanted you, that voice,
that look, reddish hair,
acting through the teeth of despair, lunacy, longing,

or soft russet animal that anyone would believe,
take home, feed and set free.

Travel

Hypnotized

She could have been a department store clerk
at the cosmetics counter.
Curls sprayed, woman I've hired
to send me into a trance.

I'm an insomniac and have paid her
to force entry into the room of sleep.
In the first half of the $120 hour,
we chat and she deduces I am a sensitive person.

But from afar, I watch myself start to buy in.
White noise hums behind the velveteen recliner.

Her curls dissolve in the dim lamp.
I fall in love with her voice,
smoke through padded headphones.

Go somewhere safe, says the voice.
I fly to the artist hills of Wimberley, Texas,
where I visited a friend I loved
for her alert expression, well rested.

Her clay tile cabin leans into the wide creek
swimming along the top of the lone star,
rowboats float by, trees linger knee deep ...

Suddenly the hour is up
and the trance maker ushers me back.
Walking out of the ordinary-looking office building,

I check my pockets for grains of evidence
that something has changed.
That night I stride into the bedroom,
swinging my new upper hand.

Sleep considers staying the night.

Beard's Fork, West Virginia

The fork slides into the mountain like warm pie.
A church at the end of one tine.

Minister comes twice a month Sundays.
Doctor sets up clinic second Fridays.

One single-lane road dead ends
at the door of Southern Appalachia forest.

Artie slopes his shoulders under his soft t-shirt.
Black among 20 whites who've
never seen this holler.

He looks us over,
his "Global Volunteers" of the week.

We are sleeping bags and back packs,
California, Texas, Minnesota and Kansas.

Work gloves and hammer,
Pennsylvania and New Hampshire.
Inside the green mountain, it's coal black.

Artie assigns us
to three housing sites inside the fork.

We break rocky soil for new apartments.
I stand, useful, inside a real tool belt,
leather loop snug around my wood-handle hammer.

Pink foam insulation gun in my tiny right hand.
Brown bandana
around my forehead in 90 degrees of heat.

Gratefully, a crew of young men,
hired by the "Youth Build" jobs program,
comes to help.
Youth-build Mac works in his holler of a body,
cigarette smoke and sweat shine.

Tattoo writing
a vertical
story
of labor
down
his back.

Watching Improvisational Theatre from a Bench in Parc La Fontaine, Montreal

The trunk lies howling with smoke
in a dry pond of sand, stones,
scraps of litter, a broken fountain.

A burning piece of forest
on its back asking for water.

And here comes the large red truck,
yards of hoses, and six alert men
assembling themselves high on the hill,

like caped industrious vigor,
in ridiculous proportion.
As if the whole house was aflame.

Water springs arc de triomphe,
white and gray rainbow of glass
to hush the pest of tree scrap,
no bigger than a cupboard.

The prone trunk looks asleep now
in its own damp pool.
Yet is whispers, like a dead man,
I'm still here: I'm a raft, a raft!

The shoots of temporary water shrink
into small wet sticks,
the fire truck rolls away,

and I imagine rain enough
to lift a broken arm of tree
and float a world of drought into the next century.

Elegy to a Daughter

Her mouth opens before the moon arrives,
full of dust.
Her small girl and boy, blinking fawn,
ride the knees of their grandmother,

who can play the harp,
but it is not the sound of their mother.
She is riding a broken deer toward the moon.

Small hearts, not knowing
they will open and close on the hinge
of this morning. In a room
where someone touches their mother's chin

to close her mouth. The grandmother
weeps as she sweeps dust
under the bed, applies color to her daughter's lips,

holds her daughter's slack shoulders
to wrap them in a flowered blouse.
The moon arrives as usual, like a moon would.

One deer crosses a road. Another one doesn't.
One song rides in the woods,
another crawls along the dust on the floor,
wrapped in the ghost of joy.

for Bernadette

The Safe

In a corner of their bedroom,
my grandfather hid his money in a safe.

Their plain house sat on a rise of ground in Lisbon,
North Dakota, along the wild Sheyenne.

He spent his days on the bench choosing sentences
for injustice brought on Ransom County.

I imagine Grandpa George
most often heard stories of theft.
Or once in a while a burglary,
someone imagining they could crack
one of these quiet houses and take something.

River valley, his horses
poked at sweet grass in a rented field,
old leather saddles thrown over their backs.

After supper he rode alone,
or on occasion with a kid from Lisbon
who agreed to climb up for a ride.
Two horses along the fence.

In summer he hoisted me onto a horse's back,
what I loved about visiting him,
coming all the way from Minneapolis.

At home he spoke little,
at times a face of grief, at other moments

picking up his violin on top of the piano,
to play a slow, original melody.

x

George's second wife, Grandma Toots,
hid diamond earrings
in the back of her drawer.

The summer I was old enough to visit on my own,
she reached into the drawer one afternoon.
George at the courthouse.

I had just confided to Toots,
as we sat alone on the bed,
that freshman year was marked by my tragic fall

for a funny, redhead English major.
A young man who loved literature
but would never love a woman.
Grandma's voice sunk to whisper:

Don't tell your friends in Minneapolis—
there's your reputation to think about.
I didn't tell her Minneapolis could care less.

But I took the comfort she offered
from two half carats in a velvet box,
blinking behind an old tangle of stockings.

His money remained stashed unto his death,
crouched in the dark metal compartment
enclosing, I imagine, memory of the double loss
of fetus and first wife, when it wasn't safe.

When George died, Grandma hired a safe cracker.
Because someone pries
the locked boxes of old men, I sit in a pretty house.

But the living room is dark.
No way to crack the code on light.
I turn the lock often,
hoping for the click of an opening.

Graduation

Eight of 15 show up.
Women who stood curbside,
service for the car rolling down Lake Street,
the lake growing smaller,
as the car rolls toward the river.

Passenger window down, *hey baby.*
His voice is small,
floats through the interior of the car
past the rear view mirror, out the open window,
invisible in street noise. *Let's go for a ride.*

x

This time eight get certificates for the journey—
arrest to sentence,
workhouse to support group, 12 meetings.
Sheet cake on a table, balloons suspended,
purple and white faceless heads,
not asking for a thing.

Keynote speaker carries herself, 70 and heavy
to the front of the room, clutching
a tiny dog like a little girl.
We didn't have programs like this.
She's written a book, 16-year-old new mother,

no money, standing on the curb.
It only takes 10 minutes
looking like you got no place to go
until the car pulls up. *Hey baby.*

She supported the baby in Hollywood, in Vegas,
on movie star customers, who danced soft shoe.

x

Young mom takes her turn next,
11-year-old daughter sitting in the back.
Tells us she wished
she'd gotten herself together sooner,
for her girl, but doubts
she would have made it this far without her.

Another one stands, twisting
a small plastic bag from Walgreens.
Pulls out scented candles as she speaks,
gifts for her PRIDE advocates
Artika and Shantae, Athelene and April,
from Prostitution to Independence,
Dignity and Equality.

She gives each candle a light kiss,
inhales the vanilla, the cinnamon,
before handing them over.
She wants to give them something
for being there when she was in court
trying to get her kids back,
giving her permission to believe she is somebody.
Artika stands behind each graduate,
strings a silver pendant around each one's neck.
Pride floats through the room
like fingers in our hair.

x

Last woman to stand, didn't make it
to enough sessions to graduate.
Just here to say thank you.
She's different from a few weeks back
in Thursday morning group,
taking my journaling class,

when her long hair was falling over a pretty face,
telling us when she was molested by her father,
hoping it all would've changed
when she was adopted.

Now she stands in men's clothes,
shaved head, so thin and flat
she might pass for a man
but for the long, natural eyelashes.
She apologizes for missing group,
explains the john beat her up,
kept her locked in a small room.

But she's back, ready this time in long gray pants,
and heavy men's shoes
to keep her walking past the roll of the car.

for PRIDE, a service of The Family Partnership, Minneapolis

Every Four Days

A 15-year-old mother stabs her newborn boy,
stuffs the body inside the duffel bag.

Young father
dumps the bag in a water quarry in Ohio.
Four-pound package sinks like chill.

Buried in water and stones,
found six months later,
diver exploring the quarry floor.

Oprah interviews tearful mother in prison.
Hid the pregnancy, eating little
to keep her belly small.

Every day in America a parent
murders their child, newborn to teenage,
every four days a newborn is found dead
in a public bathroom, in the trash,

in the woods, young mothers running through trees,
tiny mouths flying through their hair like bats.
Every four days.

With gratitude for health care providers of contraceptives, preventing
unwanted pregnancies, preventing endangered children, and for "safe
haven" laws in every state, allowing an anonymous hand-off of an
unwanted infant at a safe location. The sources on filicide (when
parents kill their children, newborn to grown) are the U.S. Bureau of
Justice Statistics and research in the Journal of the American Medical
Association.

Pushing the Creek

In the morning the old blue carpet
in the boy's room was the ocean,
rocking ships, little plastic knights
along the shore, horses and capes,

capturing and saving,
playing the pendulum of the human swing.

In the afternoon he wanted his small body
in real water,
in the fast crooked offspring of the river.

As a girl I would dangle sticks in this creek,
but not jump in
until today. Water pushing east,
the boy decides to push west.

Dragging inner tubes against the mighty Minnehaha
I wrap a hand around his forearm.
His fingers cling to my wrist.

O, but could the river of children
conceived unwanted be dammed.
So I pretend my boy and I are the world.

The creek sucks at the soles of our rubber shoes.
Nearly pulls them off our curled toes.

Until we give into the current, carried in one piece.

Gifts of Blue

Found a loose blue denim shirt
soft as thread

off the free table at a church
worn in by a bigger woman

fold up the sleeve cuffs
let go in powder blue

remember sleep
in this blue

notice tall grass at dusk
bends yellow
blue.

Pearls

Mother found dead less than 48 hours ago,
buried quickly at the bottom of the cemetery valley,
I am in the house, opening each drawer.

I've always loved this bedroom
since her mother died,
leaving her money for the hardwood floor,
white and blue petal wallpaper and curtains.

Powder breathes from the top drawer
of her heavy wood dresser,
where the platinum wedding band
is buried in powder.

White gloves. Further back, behind scarves,
a long blue velvet box.
Donaldsons in silver letters,
printed on satin inside the lid.

I hold the pearls, cool stones in my hand.
I don't how they came to her,
or when she wore them.

I'll create the scene now.

Alive, standing in front of me,
hardly taller than my 5 feet, her hair short and dark,
back facing me, I string them
around her neck. Without seeing her face

I feel the quick inhale
of her body receiving these pearls.
I turn her around;
she's smiling on the arm of someone proud of her.

I hold the pearls another minute.
Lay them back in the soft box. Close the lid.

Occasionally I wear the pearls,
beauty around my neck,
remembering the bed where she was found,

two steps from the pearls in the back of the drawer.

Waiting

There were days my mother would leave the house
and return arms full of triumph.

She would walk pussy willows through the door,
soft fingertips,
buds that are complete,
don't have to become something more.

Willows that I believed, like a story,
were borne in separate stems,
received by the wrapping of soft paper,
in buckets at the grocery store.

In this city, buildings and trees
have learned to live together,
like a painter and forest keeper
drawing the shape and color of each other.
Green canopy street, white clapboard,
front porch. Refuge of art.

One day the city forest confers among itself,
like concerned cousins,
and proffers me the real deal on pussy willows:
They are not your stock flower
below the knee; they come from trees.

Smaller than an oak or maple,
the pillars of city trees.
Still, the pussy willow is a sturdy tree,
standing on this corner like a bus catcher,
a lemonade seller, something from childhood.

The willows stop me on my walk,
look at me eye level. *Grown daughter,*
welcome, before you is an entire tree of us.
Waiting for you to notice.

A willow releases
into a girl's hand from the stick whole,
broken off without a snap, without a sound.

Never crumbles like a frail petal, leaf, no,
firm and buzzing in the fingers,
the bee who doesn't sting.

Something to carry in a pocket,
will not wilt or crush,
when a room is tottering, keeps all of itself intact.

The tree is standing here like it's nothing,
like it has its place in the forest,
like trees with real leaves and color, dressed to kill,

branches that stretch and stay poised,
without bend at the end,
without droop, the dancer's stretched hand,
the pointed toe.

A tree to plant for the duration, not waiting
until someone else brings something
blooming through the door,

she is buried in a green valley in the city,
I am who I am waiting for now.

Conducting at 13

I ride the bus to the University of Minnesota, then walk across the sprawling campus to a music hall where young people are learning to conduct orchestras. We are a summer class of 16 irregular teenagers in love with classical music. One of us is a boy quite short, cherub face. Another is a tall girl with a mop of black curls falling down her head. The music room is hot. Smells of old sheet music.

Henry Charles Smith, associate conductor of the Minnesota Orchestra, asks us to choose a movement the orchestra knows well. But cautions he will instruct the orchestra members to play it as we conduct them. I pick Schubert's "Symphony No. 8 in B Minor (Unfinished)" for my first conducting debut. (By the fall, I am a "seasoned" conductor— one season, but who's counting—and pick the more subtle "Symphony No. 40 in G Minor" by Mozart.) At home I put the record on my turntable. Sit criss-cross on old stubbly blue carpet in the living room, facing the record player, my summer-long best friend. I clutch the white tapered innocent stick. The music becomes scratchy after weeks of playing hours every day, but my grasp of the score becomes sharp.

I hear this music as I walk, my hand drawing triangles in the air for 3-beat measures. Mr. Smith tells us great conductors know the music down to the second. Ask Stanislaw Skrowaczewski how long is a movement of Beethoven. He can note the time, walk away, eat his lunch, playing the movement in his head, check his watch again, and come back to report exactly how long.

As conducting students we get free Friday night tickets to the orchestra at Northrup Auditorium. Mom and I dress up and sit near the back. Discreetly, I conduct with my hand from my seat, losing track of who or what is making music—the musicians, instruments, the conductor's stick, or my own hand.

At the end of six weeks it is our day to stand before the fully assembled Minnesota Orchestra. The press is in the house. Parents and friends sit in the dark audience. When it's my turn I walk up to the stage, nervous, stick gripped in right hand. To help myself concentrate, I unconsciously glue my tongue to my upper lip. The Minneapolis *Tribune* photographer captures that strategic move on my part. The photo accompanies the story for the Picture magazine section in the paper. Mom will save the image in a scrapbook.

I raise the stick and, like soldiers, every member of the orchestra quickly straightens themselves in their seats, raising their instruments in a crisp, simultaneous salute. I am shocked at the power I now realize I possess in my right hand. I press down on the open spine of the small, mustard yellow score book to keep it in place on my podium. I've marked every page with conductor's notes. I know this music. I bring down the stick to strike the first beat: bass clef B, on cello and violin, and Northrup instantly fills with Schubert. As the movement flows, musicians alternate their attention between the music on their stands and up to me, their conductor, deferentially watching my stick for tempo, and my left hand for expression.

Still recovering from the power of my right hand, I shock myself again at what my *left* hand can do. At the first crescendo I open my left palm—as Mr. Smith has taught us—and begin to raise it slowly above my shoulder. My heart nearly stops as this orchestra instantly obeys, their eyes glued to the pace of my rising super hand, music swelling louder and louder, matching my unspoken command.·

As I create crescendo out of thin air in one hand, I don't lose the steady 3/4 beat produced by the stick in my other hand. When the volume reaches the height that Schubert probably would have wanted at this moment, I turn my palm down and begin to lower my hand. The musical subjects before me immediately follow my decrescendo. We all are lowered from the clouds back to the worn hardwood floor. Nothing gets better than this. When it's over, I turn and make a quick bow to the applause. The next kid conductor walks up. Sweaty score of Bizet's "Carmen," and formidable stick, in hand.

Why I Love Handel's Messiah and the Hallelujah Chorus Sing-Alongs

The unpaid sopranos
    two octaves above our heads
who lift the room
special woolen sweaters safely strapped
to their bosom.

   and the government of good
   upon our shoulder

My mother, Jewish atheist, rising from floor
to piano bench, making messiah from scratch.

   Her *King of Kings* and *Lord of Lords*

   Her smoker's *Hal-*
   le-lujah

On my annual blind date with Jesus
I am Basilica people.

   won-der-ful, coun-sel-lor

From the cold parking lot downtown
car grease pasted on concrete
we hunch in our coats

daughters and
princes of peace

skitter along the sidewalk in boots
(and the crazies

in high heels) staccato
up shallow steps

push through doors built for giants
sing our way to unison.

The Climb

Watching out the bus window on the road
toward Pincushion Mountain,
skis bundled, the white of winter
covering the lake and flat shore.

But then we feel the tilt,
like that crook in the arm of a ballerina

in white, who rises from her dressing table,
slips her fingers into a long white glove.

It swallows the island of her hand,
then the slender trail
up her wrist just past the elbow.

Now stories above the lake, looking down,
broken ice has heaved itself into the air

and fallen into solid arms:
the dancer's catch, how clear it is

from the climb to top of the land,
where the trees are talking
of our arrival.

Morning Pancakes

Awake before my son,
before he asks me to find him his clothes,
before I pitch overhand black t-shirt

illuminated with bright footprints,
cub, kit, fawn, porcupette,

and the boxers and sweatpants,
hoping they land like pancakes
on his buttery yellow head.

Before he figures out one morning
that he is preparing to live
apart from where he started.

I spread a jazz hand
across my sleepy, retired belly,
crossing the path, thumb to little finger,

from the button where I was fed
to the first exit I offered my children.

The Present Hour

Suicide Note Revised

1)

after L.

As she sleeps in the middle of the day,
he climbs three stories,
leans over the viewer's ledge in the mall,
surveys a tiled, hard floor,
design in motion, tired legs
longing for sleep. Wheels

under babies, asleep. Hearing muzak,
recalling music,
recalling love's ripe hour. Steps onto the top

stair of the escalator. He slides past the Gap, safe,
a smooth ride down like a banister
under the seat of a young boy.

I'm picking up fresh bread.
I'll be home before dinner.

2)

after Letters to a Stranger by Thomas James, 1946-1974

In his right hand the young poet
holds the trembling
paint brush, October afternoon gold
cooking in the bristle.
The gun in his left.

By evening sits down to compose
a letter to a familiar face.
Longing life, he begins,
wagering the reasons will follow.

Runnel of gold slides down his canvas,
the sun at last dipping its color safely into the lake.

3)

The sky sits up in its hammock, slung pine to palm.
Puts down its glass of dry red,
gives the color wheel a counter-clock turn.
Slouches back to watch squash-orange leaves
turn back into summer-green again.
Decided against a crispy fall.
Hanging on to every last twig instead.

4)

Dear Ones, Changed my mind. Planning to live.

The Save

The late hour so often refuses
to see the point to calling it a day.
Last night The Martian, on television,
was the clasp around my sleepy wrist.

Matt Damon growing potatoes
to keep himself alive.
I knew how it ended, had seen the movie before,

but didn't remember just *how* he was saved,
how he flung himself into space,

grabbed that orange tether like a long tape
that measured the distance to safety.

I was up until 2 a.m. to watch that save.
This morning I am reeling myself
into bright daylight.

It Is Now Written

I dust the worn Kimball upright you hammered,
announcing somebody's messiah.

If you, at least, could be mustered,
take one look, Mom, at my boys.

You called a florist in your last June,
after I wrote I was pregnant.

They arrived tall, like branches of a small tree,
green and white in bloom, standing on our table.

Here is the black and white I've never seen,
you and Dad,
bobby socks, bride of 20. Shocked and happy.

At 49, you shook a cardboard box,
to sift your mother
into the tall pink bonnets in the back yard.

By then the house was stirred
just by you and the phone and the pale cat
I left in your lap one day,
then flew to London, 20 and light.

But there were afternoons with people who howled
at your comic, round-the-lake commentary—

the church group you tried, *We Care,*
and rechristened, *Who Cares?*

There was a walk
on that partial day you said goodbye
to whoever it was, came into the house,
climbed in bed.

The phone went ringing and ringing.
Only a policeman
looked at you under a cover, white female body, 54.

He guessed it had been two days.
Found, he wrote, *9:30 p.m.,* the last day in July.

Were you asleep when
an armless fist squeezed your heart?

As you drifted,
the sun painted rectangles in your room,
it is now written.

In bed with books and the cat. There was a breeze.
The hinge windows were swung open.

Father and Son

The father's cells drop like silent sand.
His son, not born, bends and collects

himself to make an entrance
in August. Knowing nothing

about the marrow of his father's bones.
The dying and the starting

pull their own gravity
like a third string.

From this window,
the April wind waltzes the lake,
as spring buries winter.

No One Has Told You

He's dying now, Mother.
Your son is 53. You were 54.
This would have killed you

so I can safely break it open now.
The truth on a piece of paper

like the fortune cutting its way
out of the coy, brittle cookie from China.

His wife's from China.
Their 4-year-old boy is a lovely color,
dark and light.

I don't think your son will last
as long as you did, Mom.

No one has told you
until now.

Second Grade Lunch

At Monday's lunch buffet, for $3.75,
I choose three small meatballs
in sweet red sauce, a vegetable medley,
two fresh carrot sticks,
sample one bite of canned pear,
which reminds me I can
usually enjoy store-bought canned peaches
but not pears.

I'm in line holding my cardboard tray,
molded into sections
so each species of food keeps to itself,
then wedge my adult female self
between two 7-year-old boys
seated on the laminated bench,
bolted to the long table
among a hundred second graders
across the loud cavernous room.

Sharing our short section of bench
none of the three of us is concerned
that our folded torsos brush up against each other
like assumptions. I love the boy on my right side
because he is the exquisite son
of my deceased brother.

I love the boy on my left side,
whom I have not met before,
because without hesitation
he parts the second-grade sea
to allow me in, as if I too am his old aunt
who wants to eat beside him, hip to hip,
and because this Monday's lunch company
beats all lunches in recent history.

for Richie

Ode to Wildflowers in the City

To snapdragons, toadflax, butter-and-eggs,
lion's mouth,
to the yellow snarl in September
on the hill below the house

under the orange sugar maple
planted as a comeback that year,
when Lucas was born, after the giant elm fell.

To Russian crowds of purple sage, brideweed,
lion's mouth barking back at the lawn mower,

all having breakfast after lunch, tiny margaritas
long before dinner, little happy hours before fall.

Who was it who called the city
to report weeds and tall grass?

They are not invited to parties
of large bumblebees hanging upside down,
swinging like wind, yet precise in their devour.

Cleaning the Fireplace
for the Next Dweller

One fire in 20 years
is clean in memory.

A kind man is sitting on the floor,
the heat hitting his knees.

There were marshmallows, and wine.
The next day he left a square wrapped box.

When it opened, they flew—

hundreds of tiny white ribbons
unraveled from Hershey's chocolate kingdom

of silver-dome temples,
kissing the floor like ashes.

Unpacking

I did this on purpose,
wrapped the small things without labeling them
to give myself a birthday

when I knew I'd be sitting in a new room,
opening tissue and towel like a new woman
to see what the old one wanted to keep.

From her travel across 50 years she brought me
a few of the boys' soft miniatures, a giraffe, a camel,
the tie-dye onesie from California.

The faded striped legs
of her own Raggedy Ann dangle comfortably
from a perch on the bookshelf

of poets and writers
who settle in beside each other again,
old friends for the duration.

Me Too

Eight student doctors and their teacher
surround the papered table.

They talk about the knee while they touch her calf,
the bulbous right knee itself, then her thigh, then
between her legs. Still talking about the knee.
It's 1963.

In a big university teaching hospital,
they are taught what they can do,
when a mother, told juvenile rheumatoid arthritis,
leaves the room for a few minutes.

In a warm tub at home,
the 4-year-old girl looks down at the crooked river
sewn into her knee. Then she examines
the pink parts ebbing from her body,
looking for the place doctors twisted like faucets.

The girl wonders what they found there,
to try to fix her knee,
to make it stop hurting, make it smaller,
like her left knee,
a pretty upside-down saucer.

The doctor said
the knee was swollen with hot soup.
Said he would make a small cut,
let the soup spill down the drain,
all the painful carrot pieces
she feels with her fingers under the warm skin.

When she wakes up the river is cut five inches long,
thirty pink stitches along the banks,
between fingers of infection.

She lives the next five months in children's rehab.
Deep steel tubs of heat.
Kids with floppy heads kept up by buckles.

She screams when long needles go into the knee,
but she would get upright.
Wheelchair to parallel bars.

Two crutches to one.
She would walk away from the hospital,
alive, the same limp she had going in.

Join walking children in kindergarten.
Color pink paths on construction paper.
Write her way up.

Small Favor

Jews of my history pour grape juice,
braid bread and whisper my God,
You are one.

Christians march the beat
in triplicate, here He is,
and here, and here.

I don't count you,
like the ones who know
they know you.

But no need for a word. Please
just do my favorite trick—

Pour the look of fire
into dying leaves

that always catch
my unspeakable
falls.

Anthem of Arthritis

I carry my body through a forest each day,
limbs knotted in chords
of fallen wood,
a persistent songbird of pain in the wind.

My fingers have all splayed away
as if they had a falling out with my thumbs.

I type sideways, the finger pads slanted,
hitting the letters edgewise.

In sleep pain is reduced to an inaudible hum,
loosening bramble from shoulder to wrist,
knee to toe.

Then I wake up and my fingers
still have their stubborn little heads
turned away from my thumbs.

I try to lift the hinge at my arm too quickly
and a night stick raps the joint.
Where do you think you're going, Ma'am?

In her later years, a single woman
in such condition must be her own hero.
I'll be up in a few minutes, I negotiate
with the law that rules the land, elbow to ankle.

I gird myself to walk to the kitchen,
eat something small and quick
which becomes a tiny life raft for today's pill
to jump on, and row itself into my blood.

Then the day folds like a robe in a house
that loves me, by evidence of running water
and refrigerated food.

The white pill, missile shape, gives me six hours,
the next day's blue oval will give me 12.

Today during my remission
I take my son for a haircut,
find a chair in the waiting area
to watch this young man,

his head in her hands, combing his dark blond hair,
once the color of sunlight,
and catch snippets of their conversation.

He is going to college in the fall.
Information I already have
but just to hear his voice in the world is a song.

Not unlike the lyric of a graceful, heroic tree
in a forest of welcome.

They Left the Flag

Moving in, I see it hanging
on the right side of the house
waving to the rust-red shutters.

It flutters above the red cuts of decorative metal
which lie like spent swords
along the hinges of the garage door.

Weathered white stripes
nod to the birch in front of the master window.
It enjoys the wind

like I do, getting wrapped like a gift,
and flapping about a conversation
I intend to have with the stars.

National Night Out, Stillwater, Minnesota

I knock on all 25 doors of my
new block of people in Stillwater,
immigrant from the big city.

I don't know you, I'm not selling anything,
but will you come out of your house,
stand in the street

some of us strangers, a Tuesday night in August,
like people do in Minneapolis and Milwaukee?

I've gone to City Hall and asked for barricades,
I like to add,
showing my resourcefulness,
hoping it will carry the appeal of a neighborly pie.

Our folding tables will hold hamburger hotdish
and cheese dip,
and the barricades will prevent the kids,
riding loops on their bikes,

from being run down in the middle
of Maryknoll Drive on our designated night,
I continue on, a knowing veteran
of all things block party.

A fire truck and police car will arrive at 7:30
on our Night Out.
Officer Dan will bring toys and the children

can climb the red truck like a sturdy oak tree
because there will be no fire to stop,
no crime to interrupt, no rescue to make.

I am carrying my homemade fliers and clipboard
and pen, writing down all my neighbors' names,
and pertinent details to get the story,
like the efficient newspaper reporter I once was.

Young Armenian Lev and wife Stacy
moved in this year.
Geoff and Leah and kids are home from their
mission, bringing back a baby from Namibia.
Greg is finally getting married
and kicking out the roommates.

I arrive at the brown one-story
of a woman who looks older somehow than her
middle-aged face. I give her a flier, with its inviting
phrases in alternating in red and black
like stripes—Join us. Bring a lawn chair.
Night to Unite. (What they call it here.)

The woman at the door tells me
her husband has died.
I look into her fearful eyes.

I had reached her doorstep walking
up a freshly constructed wheelchair ramp.
A safe gradual rise with a flat rest in the middle,
before it goes the distance to her door.

She is glad I am at her threshold, listening to her
recite the details about this ramp
that was built for him. To be polite,
she says she'll come to the party.

She does not want a Night to Unite.

But it's all I have to offer a new widow, with a ramp
that never heard his wheels clatter up and down.
A party I say, knowing I should have attended
the funeral if I had met her before today.

I hope you will come, walk down these wooden
planks to the rest of us, a ramp not meant for you,
still up on your own legs, like mine, that climbed
the new slope to meet you.

The Neighborhood Loses a Daughter

To a reckless driver,
and the dust is not allowed to rest.

Her mother uses a tiny paint brush
to get to the crevices
of each ornament on the living room shelves.

On the back deck over her garden,
inhaling a half-cigarette by the hour,
she quietly minces her lungs.

This summer she added a pond
for plump orange fish
the color of Wendy's hair.

By fall, over the fence, I notice her
carefully scoop each one out
before winter freezes them.

She asks after my children.
Then ponders aloud, *one fish missing,*
might it have been snatched by a bird?

I imagine a white osprey circling our trees.
Glint of orange catching his hungry eye.

   for Susan

Ending the Affair with the Lake

The pond behind the new house said
make your footprints on my winter back,

as it hides half its body in the forest.

We'll figure it out from here,
said the pond,

sounding almost like the lake,
behind the old house in the city.

I'll move wind through floating-glass
summer water.
I'll sound like a chime you've heard before,
said the pond.

I'll wait until you canoe across the city's wide,
pretty lake.

Let you come around to the nighttime orchestra
of pond frogs, the garage-band racket

of a hundred ducks suddenly summoned
by the welcoming sky.

Marriage Epilogue

His door was always closed,
the hallway then always dark.

After a long while I no longer wanted him
to come out of his room.

But I missed his window.
The maple tree
shared the light with him for eight years,

watched him, knew what he was doing.
Now that he's gone I think of asking the maple,

What did he look like?
But then I think again.

Instead I stand at the window
to introduce myself, pleased to meet you.

Summer of Mine

You cut out on me today,
had me pulling the red fall jacket
over my chilly arms in July,
I hate you for that.

Where exactly did you go?
Whose bare-arm skin soaked you in
like butter melting under a sunny side up egg.

I never had a real affair
in those long, long years of marriage.
Never betrayed either, quite like that.

I was born in your month of July
and I know you love me for it.
Innocent and warm, you quietly meet me
on the deck in the back every year.

You are the one I run away with.
No one notices us canoe across the pond,
no one knows
you are mine alone.

Brief Mysteries

On a warm night in a parked car,
unplugged dash, telling a story,

making one bend into laughter,

the laugh pealing out the window
into the sleeping neighborhood,

whites of eyes in dark bedrooms blink,
thinking, screech owl?

The Understudies

Were one to commission
a biographer on her behalf
it would be noted that she often finds herself
counting to three:

Two sons and herself, a joyful three.

A three-member family of origin,
two children, one parent.
Three attempts at the storied two-parent family,

the marriage of her parents,
then her own two marriages
falling like three sickly trees in the family forest.

But in her sixth decade
the dense trail suddenly opens
onto a waving summer field.

Standing there is her youngest son,
brown eyes lit upon her, and his girl,
long blonde hair swaying slightly, like strands falling
from the willow tree in her own backyard.

Standing in for the two fairy tale parents,
the understudies arrive
from behind the trees just in time
to reach the old wooden stage.

She knows he's only 18, his love just 17.

Nonetheless, biographer, pronounce us
a whole family at last.

Reading the Instructions
of Derek Walcott

Give back your heart to itself, he said,
to the stranger who has loved you all your life …

This heart searched for itself
for decades, peering into the dark dust

a head beneath the bed cover,
a face burrowed in a chair,
lit by a television screen.

Threw away letters,
wedding cards, the first diamond ring

pushed across the glass counter for cash,
the stones in the second plucked out

to become white sparks
upon my ears, fingers free from the gold clasp.

Was finally located
in the smooth chest of a small boy,
then another,

each beginning in the chamber
just below the heart,

hearing the beat of it,
a sound I had never heard.

This summer the last son
moves into his own home.
This heart is falling into that chamber below,

like a slippery handful of dough
I can't shape into something buoyant.

I believe I am telling myself

this is where the stranger steps in.
Reaches into that chamber.
Holds the space until the last beat.

After Derek Walcott's poem "Love After Love"

The Receiving Quilt

Receive: "to greet or welcome"

Pedaling the black iron treadle of the old Singer,
a grandmother
stitched a small square quilt of colors to receive
the granddaughter.

The sewing machine hangs upside down in its
wooden table.
Its four narrow drawers for spools and buttons
are repurposed

into housing for small square Lego people,
who populate the world of
the granddaughter's children.

How easy it is to love children, how impossible
to save them all from harm. How that doesn't
stop this story

from speaking for them, before they exist.
A girl, a boy,
will thank their mother and father for waiting
to conceive them

until they are parents ready to receive them.
No love is more patient, no preparation more holy.

Knock until you find the supporting wall.
Conceive a welcome cup for the table.

Apply gold leaf with the gentlest fingertip.
Even a small jolt
will fracture this fragile color of promise.

Before carrying someone new, find what carries you
through the hours of the world. Consider referrals.

I know someone who knows a way to beckon
the soul into the body on Tuesday nights

from the second floor of her duplex.
How love creeps into a patchwork quilt of people

sitting in a circle in her otherwise ordinary
living room.
How it washes your hot face, drives your car
all the way home.

Acknowledgements

My poetry work has been sustained by many fine teachers and poets, to whom I am very grateful: George Roberts and Judy Daniels at Twin Cities Institute for Talented Youth; John Minczeski, Natalie Goldberg and Michael Dennis Browne at The Loft Literary Center; Thomas Swiss and Marvin Bell at University of Iowa workshops; Steve Kowit and Ellen Bryant Voigt at California workshops; Sharon Doubiago and Phebe Hanson at Split Rock Arts Program; Margo Fortunato Galt, Jill Breckenridge and Rachael Hanel at Grand Marais Arts Colony; Levi Romero at Taos Institute of Art; Michael Burkard at Provincetown Fine Arts Work Center; and Joyce Sutphen at Stillwater Library's workshop. I am indebted to the inspiring teachers at Hamline University's graduate writing program: Barrie Jean Borich, Deborah Keenan, Jim Moore, Patricia Weaver Francisco, Juliet Patterson, Larry Sutin, Sheila O'Connor, Mary Rockcastle, and Katrina Vandenberg, thesis advisor; as well as Kate Green, supplemental thesis advisor. Thank you to my nurturing writing group: poets KateLynn Hibbard, Morgan Grayce Willow, Rondi Atkin and Rita Schweiss. Thank you to my supportive writing students, friends and family including Dawn Cottle, Richard Cottle, Sue Henderson, Fran Cottle, Judy LaVercombe, Tulie Schumacher, Tracie Bergeson, Lynn Woodland, Jesse LaVercombe and Lucas Schumacher. And many thanks to the kind, discerning Tom Driscoll, publisher of Shipwreckt Books!

The Receiving Quilt poems "Elegy to a Daughter," "Rear View Mirror," and "They Left the Flag" were previously published in the *Nodin Poetry Anthology*; the poem "Lake Harriet" was published in *Between The Lakes - The Poets of Linden Hills* and *Tipton Poetry Journal.*

Other poems of mine have been published in *Main Channel Voices*; *Minnesota Poetry Calendar*; *Southwest Journal's* poetry pages; and *rock, paper, scissors*, Hamline University's student journal.

About the Poet

Elissa Ann Cottle lives in Stillwater, Minnesota. She has been teaching Creating a Writing Life since 2004, a private class for adults to write poetry, memoir or fiction, held at ArtReach St. Croix in Stillwater, and on Zoom. Since 2010, she has produced When Writing Meets Art, a literary and play reading series, currently held at Stillwater's Zephyr Theatre where she is the literary arts director. She is also the editor of the Stillwater *Gazette's* literary page, Valley Muses. She is a consultant and editor for individuals pursuing creative work, and a writer and website designer for businesses and nonprofits. (artfulbusinesswriting.com).

She's also an advocate for pregnancy prevention to avoid unwanted children. Elissa grew up in Minneapolis. She earned a bachelor's degree in journalism and political science from the University of Iowa. For 30 years she was a newspaper reporter in California and Minneapolis, with stints in Duluth, Rhode Island, Washington, D.C., and London. She was conferred a Master of Fine Arts in Writing from Hamline University. Above all Elissa is a fortunate mother of two sons, and a devoted aunt.

Made in the USA
Monee, IL
21 September 2021